T5-BAR-545

CSU Poetry Series XLV

Daniel Bourne

The Household Gods

Cleveland State University Poetry Center

Copyright © 1995 by Daniel Bourne

Published by the Cleveland State University Poetry Center
1983 E. 24th St., Cleveland, OH 44115

ISBN 1-880834-13-8

Library of Congress Catalog Card Number: 94-69643

The Ohio Arts Council helped fund
this program with state tax dollars
to encourage economic growth,
educational excellence and cultural
enrichment for all Ohioans.

Acknowledgments

Grateful acknowledgment is made to the following publications in which some of these poems first appeared.

Alaska Quarterly Review: "Recovering"
American Poetry Review: "Bottom Fish"
Beloit Poetry Review: "Hiding the Knives"
Black River Review: "The Hypothetical Cancer"
Carolina Quarterly: "Once Again"
Chariton Review: "Refraction," "The Top and Bottom of Every Board in Existence"
Cincinnati Poetry Review: "Gleaning the Field (1973)"
Clockwatch Review: "Atmosphere"
Confrontation: "To a Woman Mauled in Yellowstone"
Cottonwood: "Boys Who Go Aloft"
Crosscurrents: "Wing Span"
Embers: "Fish Move the River"
Images: "Dionysus in Illinois"
Indiana Review: "Beside the Road," "Nota Bene," "Now or Never"
Kansas Quarterly: "Hunters Are Magnificent Animals"
Milkweed Chronicle: "The Night of the Empty Plate"
Minnesota Review: "From a Shipyard in a Bottle"
Mississippi Valley Review: "Draining the Jackson Pond (1965)," "Virginia Woolf's Half-Sister Laura," "Wreath"
Negative Capability: "I Hold My Family"
New Laurel Review: "Fishing," "The Heat, the Hands, the Harvest"
Northeast: "Intruding"
North Dakota Quarterly: "Elegy for the Woman Across the Street"
Pikestaff Forum: "Surviving the First Litter"
Poetry Northwest: "Aunt Linda Speaks," "Goodbye to the Poetry of James Wright Elegies," "Poetry for Physicists"
Poets On: "The Rainbow Sheep"
Prairie Schooner: "All the Philosophies in the World." Reprinted by permission of the University of Nebraska Press. Copyright 1991 by the University of Nebraska Press.
River Styx: "Dry Lightning"
Shenandoah: "Cleaning Out the Nest"
Sou'wester: "O Spam"
Spoon River Poetry Review: "Did You Know," "The Household Gods"
Sun Dog: "Etude in Black and White"
Tar River Poetry: "Unburied Shoes"
Webster Review: "Illinois Primer"
Woodrose: "Cleaning Out the Cistern"

A very special thanks to Felix Stefanile and the Sparrow Press, which published my chapbook *Boys Who Go Aloft* (Sparrow Poverty Pamphlet No. 52), in which the following poems appeared: "Boys

Who Go Aloft," "Cleaning Out the Cistern," "Fishing," "Goodbye to the Poetry of James Wright Elegies," "The Heat, the Hands, the Harvest," "The Household Gods," "Hunters Are Magnificent Animals," "In This World, Light . . . ," "In Which I Share a Gull's Knowledge of Rivers," "Salvation in the 1950s," "Stick Horse," "Surviving the First Litter," and "The Tree That Remains."

I am grateful for the fellowship and other support given to me by the Ohio Arts Council, the Lilly Library and the Polish Studies Center (both at Indiana University), and the College of Wooster. I would also like to thank Jim and Larry Judge, Chris Kearns, Margaret Meeker Bourne, Lee Harlin Bahan, Karen Kovacik, Cathy Atwood, Fred Brinker, Roger Mitchell, Cynthia Macdonald, Timothy Wiles, Maura Stanton, Charles Silver, Leonard Kress, Michael Cole, Nicholas Kolumban, Leonard Trawick, Major Ragain, and all those others whose voices have accompanied me at various parts of the path, and whose echoes you hear here.

Contents

To Carter Wheeler Bourne (1920-1974)
Not just for the man in the poetry,
but the poetry in the man.

I. Surviving the First Litter

Surviving the First Litter

From the start there is the dance. The young sow
who will eat her pigs or shifting in sleep
will crush the litter. The coupling of weight
with warmth, food with death we try to separate,
building a small pen beside her to save them.
At the bottom: a plank pulled out. The weak
can pass beyond the plop of her sagging
belly. She is always sleepy or cross.

Her young come to her constantly, like moving
corncobs and clods on the ground, like bloated
ticks clamped to her tender parts. They never learn.
One more dies the day we buy a heat lamp,
and we are always finding a piece of skin,
or a baby with hind legs broken, whose
suffering must be ended with a shovel.
Dad flings it out back in the ditch
to bury later. "She doesn't know better," he says.

We check there often. Dad bats the heat lamp away,
and it sways. We watch the huge sow-shadow
rock up and down the wall. The litter
has whittled down to one. "Damn this pig won't last
till weaning," says Dad bending down. When he scoops
it up it starts in squealing. Pink hooves point,
the legs stiffen. The grip of hands
is the first puckering fear, the first frenzy.
Dad looks at me. I look at the mother.

Boys Who Go Aloft

Boys die each day on the swingsets.
They twist the rope in and dizzy

it out like hot gorillas.
The yaw of the world around them

waits for them to jerk harder.
There is airplane to play.

To twist and shoot with their legs.
Like dots on the screen

their mothers appear. Boys signal
their dogs on the ground to take cover.

Bailing out over concrete
they touch on a branch with their toes.

They jump and mean it. Each day
they go up to earn more wings.

Their mothers call and call
their names and the names of their dogs.

Stick Horse

I put you between my legs, ride you
over the rough-mowed land by the toolshed
and pass through Texas. I explore.

I expect you to last forever.
Plastic head and painted eyes, long body, strong
as the handle on a rake. Now

my sister calls from the garden.
Come look! Horses
have sprung from the cucumbers.
They graze beside her planted knees, dirty
knees from digging.

It is time to attack, the tip
of your stick horse hoof
ticks madly along on the sidewalk.
Amigo, amigo, you chant. *These cucumber*
horses cannot last, stupid things!

Four short twigs for legs
under each pickle's belly, a stick
juts out the top and holds on
the small green head. *Pickle-brained*

like my sister, I say. *Only she*
would build something already dead.

We gallop up. My little whickering spike,
you whip through her pickle-horse herd

and head back toward Texas. She's crying,
calling you names and I say over my shoulder,
it serves you right when you get in our way.

O my stick horse. You will last, you will last!

The Heat, the Hands, the Harvest

The difficult slip into sleep.
Out in the fields the whirring
steel gray combines
sweep headlights through the night,
combing the tips of wheat
for the only gold
you will ever know.
There is a moan
to your toss and turn.
The combine churns
beneath his precious hands.

They brought my cousin's hands in
wrapped in a sack. He was lucky
someone came by in time
and one hand could be put back on.

There is a sag to the mattress
after midnight, to his side
of the bed. He's back . . .
Through your sleep you think
that he might kiss you. He does,
on the back of the neck, but does
no more. Harvest is far
from over. You turn
to face him, to smooth
his clenched hands
by placing them on you.
But, chin scratching
your chest, he drifts off
before you know it,
his left arm mooring
on your side.

They brought the Stacey boy in.
Found him run through the tractor
mower. It seems he hit a stump
with his back wheel and overturned.

Even with him here, dreams
will mangle. You see his old
three-wheel tractor rear up
at plowing. The duroc gilts
going wild at the scent
of blood on a cut finger.
The polled bull threatening
with the blunt hammer of his head
to foreclose on the herd and fields
he loans you each day. There is
the frantic call and rush
to the pasture.

It wasn't till my father
stopped by that they were found.
A faulty furnace
and they went to sleep and never woke up.

Cutting through the stillness
of a closed house, air conditioner
just kicked off, the stab
of a screech owl's human wailing
wakes you both.
Shivering, you call for covers.
Cover me, you say
and only then settle down
to sleep and expect a morning.

Cleaning Out the Cistern

when my mother took lunch to my father
they tied me in the shade so
I wouldn't croak on the Fitch Place
there was an uncovered well and they worried
I'd wander off to the ghosts of fallen-
in children whining "come play with us
inside"
        I whimpered the day my father
disappeared down a ladder I was certain
dropped to hell I saw my sisters
solemnly arrange the chunks of charcoal
from the filter on the grass
the pump in the kitchen gushing
dirty brown my mother's arms
surging on the handle pumping out
water stored too long inside
the noise of my father's bucket
tolling faraway he scrubbed the walls
I stood on the porch waiting
for the awesome rite to end
I was told that rain falls clean
and charcoal eats the sparrow
shit and shingle grit in the gutter
but a little gets by
           one day
second-grade Ricky said to me
"rain is poisonous" I had drunk it
all my life was troubled I told
my father that evening he mumbled
not to worry that we would clean
the cistern come spring but I dreamed
in the night of his foaming
at the mouth in the rain and his dying

16

Hiding the Knives

Hefty Clarence, our neighbor, got drunk and went
blind on wood alcohol when he was young,
a cook at the state hospital in Anna. Now he kept
getting sent back there. Brick wall and stormy,

roaring down the road he'd go, white cane ticking
the gravel. "Hide the knives," my mother would yell
when Clarence's son Raymond came loping up
bloody-nosed and whining, "Pop's gone crazy again."

Hide the knives in my bedroom, old Clarence
never climbed our stairs, wouldn't know where
they were if he kicked in our flimsy backdoor.
"We'll take off through the field," we said, "if he

turns up our lane." It was just a game
but later on the bus Raymond would get even
tossing my cap out the window for hiding the knives
till we all got too old to act that way and I

bought a hand-tooled wallet from Clarence for ten dollars
for my Dad to unwrap on his last Christmas, when
Jim and I bought Micrin mouthwash and drank it
behind Krogers' trash bins but didn't go blind

or crazy but still there were plenty of knives to hide
the sharp ones to end the dull waiting to hide
either under the mattress or in the junk on the floor
till in one dream old Clarence finds his way upstairs.

"It's a dream," I shout. "No knives in here,
just like love, they go away." But Clarence
mutters, "They're just hidden, boy. Give me time,
give me time, and I'll find them."

Salvation in the 1950s

the sweet thick liquid
the color of pee in a dixie cup
we drank this our most holy
of communions the long solemn rows
in the high school gym as children
throughout the county filed through
to gaze at the plastic cup and swallow

except for the already tainted ones
who did not come their muscles
already ruined like a crop standing
in a low-lying field under water
until browned and rotten these unsaved souls
guilty of cold baths on warm nights
or taking a swim and sitting by the fire
tried reading quietly in their seats
on Monday as the pulse of healthy kids
beat around them the excitement
of the miraculous yellow wine
offered to all who would come drink

back in the Bible cripples waited
by the roadside for the breath of the Savior
to blow their crutches away
and lift them up in the air
but nothing like this ever happened
to the boys in Olney Illinois
one day not showing up for school
and returning a year later with a leg
strapped to a creaking post of metal
they swiveled on their hips up and down
torturing their armpits on the worn
foam rubber of their crutches
exercising the chafed red balls of their hands

(and Danny Wright went with his mom
to the last tent meeting in southeast Illinois
the preacher's hands clamped down
like one more piece of iron
on Danny's limp thigh muscles the pain
all eyes of the tent on him

as the preacher let go
with his grip but not his words
Danny lunged out
toward the edge of the stage
and the sawdust landed
with a sharp burst into his mouth
"for ten minutes no one picked me up,
by then, most of the crowd had gone,"
he said and another kid asked
why hadn't the vaccine done him
any good)

but thirty years later I realize
neither Jesus nor Jonas Salk
could have helped but the sin
is that we didn't help either just left them
behind each day with our discarded clothes
before we lined up for the roll call in gym
the ritual of hot breath and flexed muscle
the study for the priesthood of health

Dionysus in Illinois

Crazy & rich this man smelled of his hobby
a wagon rolling down Route 50 with two lanes
of goats around the rim they were the reindeer
of summer harnessed with bells some pulling some
tagging along in their laziness honest the goat man
we came to see when he camped near Bonpas Creek
they say lived in the Carolinas left each May
with his baby billy & nanny goats loping
along a route through Little Egypt he traveled
no stranger than the white squirrels our county
seat claimed as fame to put on postcards he came
with his goat-powered cart & hard oak staff
like a sceptre in his hand he herded his nickering
court quivering tails & hooves hitting on the hollow
highway more empty in the 50s but motorists still
killed a few he buried them by night in the forest
& danced they said like an Indian out of sorrow
on their graves he never learned to keep them in
one lane they sprawled from ditch to ditch
like shadows before oncoming cars most of which
slowed down some stopped to watch & when the goat man
ate his lunch we kids all taunted him
"goat sandwich" we said as he raised his bread
no one ever saw him set foot inside a store
& our fathers mumbled the good they'd do
with his money on their farms but the police
let him pass as if he did have
the joint backing of coin and craziness this ripe old
man we herded ourselves around I remember
as the first sighting of Pan or Dionysus in
the Illinois countryside he invaded from the east
each spring & the kids all wanted to go with him
eat goat sandwiches & dance on graves in moonlight
like Indians till the time he didn't come so one
more dream of childhood got too ripe in the sun

and withered and now I see his worn gray staff lying
in the basement of a Carolina Colonial 50 miles
from the nearest goat but underneath the feet
of his nearest living relatives who talk about
crazy old uncle & wonder where he went each spring
when he took off with his shaggy army
well he visited me to show me my first hole
in the fence but to them the smelly & salty old goat
man is better off dead they say as they pray
for his soul though I would gladly sacrifice
all the white squirrels in the world to hear
what was born in his mind from this music made
with goats this touch of the Dionysian romp
outside the pen of my Illinois childhood & though
I was taught the sheep & goats in church the ones
herded to heaven & the ones herded to hell
I always rooted for the ones who broke loose
let white sheep and white squirrels flourish underneath
God or city ordinance but in my own myth send down the swoop
of the eagle who spares only the shaggy goat
its claws can't hold the thickly-matted fur
can't reach the smelly flesh

Illinois Primer

they interfered with business blind mice
in a nest inside the cornplanter my father's boot
took care of them stomped in shed gravel
stomped in sacrifice to spring planting I cried
you killed the baby mice killed them and Taffy
my spayed protectoress snarled at my father
as he spanked me two or three times with a stick because
I wouldn't shut up but the next day I laughed as Taffy
dragged silent yellow kittens around the yard
the scruff of their necks a tooth hold
and I laughed I too did my share of damage
swinging cats by the tail until a fang
opened up my finger

I played tug of war the rope
twisted through Taffy's teeth she was
my one true enemy as she growled and pulled one day
I watched her dig up a mole killing our yard
she wallowed it between her paws
right before it died for the first time in its life
it was making a sound and that same summer
I heard my father curse his arm got pinned
beneath the share of the three-bottom plow he was working on
he called for me to come and my adrenalin
surged up like blood to free him

but by then I could hear the cries of everything
there was Taffy circling the harvest
each year till she slowed a step and got caught
in the path of the cornpicker and died there was
my father who got caught in the web
of cancer and the doctors who said that his screams
must not be admitted (especially to him) and even though
I cried when I buried Taffy I couldn't
at my dad's funeral and now I can't
cover up in my sleep it's my dad who is yelling not dogs
not mice not anything but dad and me trying
to shake myself awake before I confess I know he is dead
that he has to leave the house

Fish Move the River

Fish move the river.
They carry it on their flexible backs.

A god thinks
a fish can live in his hands.

The fish think
god
curves inward

like a swallowed hook.

I
So how are you
my slow one   immersed
for how many years?
How long since I visited

you who stayed on the farm
with the ripe smell in the bathroom
as Dad cleaned out his tubes and pouches
each morning waking
with a jerk
to find them fastened to him.

In my poems
you have always stood accused
of not loving him enough.

II
Is the moment of baptism
the coming up for air?

We're all afraid of death
want to take our own waters with us.

I would have carried you
and all your liquid home
with me. It was not far.

But swaying in the branches
a woman

who spoke in our local tongue.
She said to follow

her deeper and deeper.

III
Do you still hug the old logs
feed by the sunken stumps?
Only in dreaming I find
myself covered
by your old element.

Sometimes I struggle

and you are up the bank
calling
but won't give a hand.

Other times I see you
at the bottom of a poem

and I think
"I must save you."

But you are too small to grab.

IV
You who lived underneath the bridge
I won't be coming back
but in my bed it will always
smell like a boy has slept here.

And across the breadth of the Little Wabash bottoms
backwaters in harvest
the mourning dove's five notes
keep sounding   the ground gorged with yesterday's rain.

Is it only in myth that three names
can merge in one being
all separate   all one?

It was you who lived with my father
with a child's name Danny   not me

and when you took on new flesh
new movements he would not recognize

it was I who showed up
called by the adult names Dan and Daniel
downstream

miles from the beginning creekbed
hauling the awkward weight of the river
trying to find a place to set it down.

Fishing

Before I learned the technique a catfish on the hook
meant taking my tennis shoes off and using one as a glove
I kept his barbed fins from spiking my fingers
while my braver hand coaxed the hook from the outraged mouth
gasping out its silent threats then using the shoes as tongs
I lifted the thrashing muscle up to launch it back
I hated eating fish but the mystery of the pulsating drops
that flowed beneath the polished darkness at my feet
always enticed me to catch one precious and slippery
as if its squirm was my very first puppy my father
used to tell they caught thirty pound whiskers
in the Little Wabash when it was low trapping fish
in hollow logs and raising with ropes down in Kentucky Lake
divers looking for a drowned man saw hundred pound monsters
and never submerged again but I just snatched the little ones
hardly bigger than the hook and letting them pout and shimmer
in an alien atmosphere their red-raw gills sucking
for the air they would never find finally I lobbed them back
for them to grow bigger and more noble prey once I caught
a half-pound bluegill and keeping him latched to the hook
I yo-yoed him back and forth from the bank watching the float
like it was a blip on a radar screen and delighted with the tug
of his body on my hands until I started to feel the quivers
that he might not enjoy the sport as much as I sometimes
I took a bucket to haul the martyrs home for the amusement
of my cats at least these fish were put to good use but once
a carp swallowed the hook and I realized it was in terminal pain
as its fins twitched beside my shoe and I pounded a rock
again and again on the rubbery head to relax its misery but it
got obstinate and wouldn't die growing increasingly caked
with late summer dust and small pebbles that bubbled like tumors
on its scales and one eye turned in so as not to look from disgust
at my ineptness there must have been a vengeful water god
watching I still have nightmares reeling monsters in my sleep

Unburied Shoes

They look the same size. This left shoe
uncovered by my hoe

and my right shoe whose leather heel ripped
in the back spokes of a motorcycle

last Friday. The family story goes
that a boy with my name last century

died from a fever, hoeing in his sleep
the rows of sweet corn and butter beans, his toes

wiggling at the fierce smell of marigolds, the orange
bloom of typhoid in his veins. If only

he put the handle down he could have lived
long enough to marry, to create a boy

whose own boy would work the garden, too. Well I
haven't died yet, but I pause in the middle

of these three rows of okra, hold this rotting foot, and knock
the dirt from my own split shoe. Even though

he would be my great uncle, I think this boy
is my only child. Sixteen, I know I am pregnant,

a clump of dirt grows in my dark hidden shell.

Dry Lightning

At night we walked out to the lawn
in back of the house, and watched dry lightning.
"Down on the Ohio River, a hundred miles away,"
my father said as the sudden cracks
split the taut sky, the thunder
so far off it would never reach us.
The stars shone bright as always in drought.

Next morning, with my bat, glove and whiffle ball
I headed out to the burnt grass to play
a game with myself, swinging
and then fielding, timing the seconds
for each batter to get to first base
and how long for the throw. Living on a farm,
no friends until fall, I kept my league
statistics in a Big Chief notebook, pencil
smudging on paper made slick from sweat
and the stains of squashed insects.

That same year, turning over in the sheets'
limp cling, the beads on my skin the only moisture
in the hot hammering air of that August dry spell,
I struggled on the strange field of my body, the new use
for what I called my bat. Worried
my furtive sport would be announced to my parents,
every night in silence my hands
ignited their own dry lightning, beautiful
even though I knew
the real thing was still a hundred miles away.

Draining the Jackson Pond (1965)

After a few hours, only the flies will remain
clutched to the smelly harvest, blue bodies
on the green staring eyes. The runt fish
are left to die in the mud; baskets
of fatter fry carted to the rusted
beds of pickups, destined for the freezers
of wheat farms sprawling for miles around.

"Several times throughout the afternoon they found
a fish so big they could not believe it was alive."

Despite the gash where they slit the old pond's back
(the warm blood of summer throbbed out
and the glistening body died), years from now
no one will believe this
was a place of slaughter. The endless cycling
of tractors, scratches made between the rows,
will never turn up a bone. No markers were left.
The secret resting place
of my first ten years of life.

Refraction

During Prince Philip's War in New York
my ancestor Elizabeth fell from a tree
and crawled to the woodpile just as warriors
came to brain her mother and younger sister.

So why am I here in this East Chicago bar
trying to scalp every brain cell she saved?
I celebrate the daughter in my loins.
The way her eyes grow tense. She worries

about rape, the Russians, the awkward way
she enters the house when her parents
have given up hope of her return. She broke
her leg last week at basketball. An entire

community wants to sign the plaster on her shin.
I drink on. My daughter will be born. Stone
in the water. A girl's voice carries from the far woods.
Each ring makes the long swim to shore.

II. The Household Gods

The Top and Bottom of Every Board in Existence

The top and bottom of every board in existence
will be burnt today.
The roaches don't wait to be told
while the fat grubs
curl the prayer of their bodies.

All the books in the world are spine open on the floor.
The wind is blowing in from the window.
There is no shelf for the call number of your book.
No parquet floor to squeak as you walk, no
oak rack to hold your magazine.

We are all at the mercy of the slats in our beds.
The top and bottom of every board in existence.
If all the birds would shut up, okay,
we could get along with this heaping the fire—
each tongue, its plaque and holy foolishness.

The Household Gods

In everybody's house there is a window
no one has ever looked out of, a dog
no one has ever spotted, a cat
which cannot be cornered and put
in a sack to throw in the river.

There is one set of drapes behind which
you would not recognize your children.
There is one chair no one moves to the table.
If you walked out now and told your neighbor
he would not even interrupt his chores.

But as you check all the rooms, you realize
the shadows are from someone else's furniture,
the noise each night in the basement
keeps rising through the pipes. In a moment
the door will swing open. Your wife will call for help.

Poetry for Physicists

Imagine you are the molecule on display,
the styrofoam balls and tinker-toy bondings
holding together the universe of your body
curving in upon itself at each edge.
Imagine your wife in the next room,
sighing, as she lifts the heavy books of your poems
from her lap and clicks off the light. By the time
her eyes grow accustomed to the quick fall of night
she forgets all the names of elements
because they do not rhyme, because the periodic
table is irregular, the line-breaks strange.

Midnight. Now you are on your feet singing
as you pull each tinker-toy stick like a thorn
from your tortured side. Your skin squeaks like styrofoam,
the puncture-hole edges crumble. But you
are happy. Soon you are floating on air.
Light floods through your study and your wife asks,
"Bob, where are you?" "I am not here, Mrs. Oppenheimer,"
you whisper, feeling guilty, thinking of the mess on the floor
while she goes to get a broom, sighing again.

But you feel relaxed, balmy, the energy released from your pores
is enough to light the Great Basin for a week,
or to burn a hole in the leaf of the mother-in-law's tongue
growing from a blue pot by your atlas.
Soon you will start humming the words *mushroom, Paris,*
suitcase and *park bench.* Soon they will start to sound like a song.
The bursts of poetry you send into space will start expanding
until the length of each syllable is constant,
until the parallel lines all merge.

O Spam

Spam is the national bird of Canada—
To hear it sing in the skillet of a morning
while it musters brown eyes and a beak
from pink, plucked skin, this is the phoenix.

Spam is the barge of the Ohio—
To see it float the heavy current
of grease waterproofing its sides,
this is the chug of glory which unlocks locks.

Spam is the gashog of youth—
To guide it down State Street at 4 a.m.
and turn into a waffle bar in one piece,
this is the living forever.

Spam is the ritual of uninvolved sex—
To use it uncooked at the sink is a treat,
the squeak on a floorboard beyond the door
of the bathroom, this is the ménage à trois.

Spam is the opiate of masses—
To come in a can and be fattening,
this is the prayer in our schools,
to live like meat but more cheaply.

Atmosphere

Here between stacks of ethnic gadgets
and instant gourmet dinners, the owner reports
"Our last Punjab wok was bought yesterday,"
as if anticipating our disappointment. Glass
breaks in the back of the store, near
the Romanian crystal. She winces, cranes
her neck over the blue cash register.
"Christmas help," she says with a martyr's sigh.
But soon her fingers return to the keyboard.
The gurgle of the terminal innards
totters on the threshold of speech.
"Our next system will have a woman's voice."

As we talk, I am burping slightly, as politely
as possible. An hour ago, in a landscape
of wicker and primitive ferns, we made a trip
to the roughage trough, your name
for the salad bar, before the green pasta
and chicken livers wrapped in bacon. Our waiter
pointed at the wine from "Possum Run,"
an Indiana vineyard, and although we said no,
we nodded how good that the grape
was challenging the soybean in our state agriculture
in the same way we applaud that natural fibers
have come back, though at a higher price.

At nine the fountain stops, the lights flicker.
Cages slam down over jungle-wear displays.
"The store is closing," a hidden voice harps.
A woman races, her opossum litter of bags
flops on her hips. This is frenzy, the first
bipeds to forage in a land without sunshine or rain.

The Hypothetical Cancer

(You, who flee him, so muffled up and dark,
who hide in the chapel with the lights turned low,
know he would not hurt you for anything.)

He would not be the face at the window,
nose pressed to the glass, all pig-like and pink;
nor would he take advantage of the dark

in the icebox innards. He would not think
of his need for a small boy in the park.
He would not say bad things to the widow.

Red stripe down the bacon, a tell-tale stink,
he would not leave his thumb-print in Crisco.
He bows his head at the young girl's remark:

"I saw you each night in my daddy's drink."
For years he has crossed and recrossed his heart:
he would not be the face at the window.

The Night of the Empty Plate*

O son, your own little daddy
walks underneath the bed,
two or three coals in his mouth
to keep them warm till morning.
The horse he slaughtered stirs
in the dirt beneath the door.

Tonight, only cucumbers
in the soup, only a little fire.
The light inside an empty plate.
The rattle of an empty spoon.
He pulls and pulls on the latch
to make sure we locked the door.

O son, this house was so new
it needed blood
to slide its beams into place
and for its roof

a kind beast's spirit.
But such a foolish animal!
This one bucked in your father's sleep.
All night it plowed a crooked row.

Now they've made up.
All is forgiven.
Talk about a short memory!

But I can still hear his whistle
out of the mouth of the stone jug.

*Slavic folk belief had it that a *dziad*, a grandfather-spirit,
watched over those still alive. But until the death of the first
head of the household, a farm would be without supernatu-
ral assistance to keep the hens laying, the crops growing, etc.
In the Ukraine, they even buried a horse underneath the
threshold so that its spirit would serve in the *dziad*'s stead.
Forefathers Eve was the time for honoring these beneficent
ghosts; plates and cups were put out for them.

Recovering

I
First, you think you see him
cradled between the sharp
nipples of the crescent.

Then, each night, the moon returns
more swollen with milk.
The same time of the month, the same
month of the year. There is a cup
you leave out on the table.

But what is this ghost, its new face?
Yellow at the far edge of corn, it begins
its wasted pacing through the sky,

growing pale with the weight of your son.
In the black water of the ditch,
you see the reflection, white half-moon
of milk above the upper lip,
his body half-submerged.

II
Tonight, there are cats
threatening, mounting the trellis,
mounting each other. They wail you awake,
make you think of your baby.

Tonight, you are sure
his face looms brightest
so close to the earth.

You move to one side of the bed

So the shadow can pass
through the room undisturbed.

Intruding

Beat a table and the scissors will ring.
—Old Polish proverb

You are in the house of your children.
All day they have been bad—their grown-up toys
scattered where you need to walk,
even in the bed where they have allowed
you to spend this one night.

When they sit you down to dinner,
they will pass nothing you need.
"Just a lot of talk," you want to tell them.
This is not right, their kitchen, their flagrant way
of handling china and the prayer over herring.
They talked slurred. You never know if the door
they have pointed to leads out or in. A new switch
gets pulled and suddenly the lights go out
in the part of town where you shop, or in a part
of your brain. No use trying to stare them to death.
They will only stare some place else.

But you cannot help intruding. You have weight
which must be shifted somewhere. A knob glistens
like fruit that is fake, frozen, or in any case
stronger than fingers and teeth combined.
You open a door to the back of the house,
to the games they play with their hands.
"I did not know these were your things,"
you can say in a scrape if they come.

The last straw is the way they hug you goodbye,
leaning over toward you as if out a window.
You see the family falling, falling. The only thing
that you would save in the middle of a fire.
And here they shout so urgently—goodbye!—
meaning "This is our house," and for you to leave
as if there were not a second to lose.

Elegy for the Woman Across the Street

They show you the dark spot on the x-ray
as if they are furnishing an estimate for your roof—
cheaper to fix if you do it right away
while there is a special on materials and labor.

Going outside, you grimace at the sudden blazing,
the sun too hot for November. Even the air
inside your car seems baked. You reach for your sunglasses,
brush through the dust on your dashboard.

The town glides by almost normal. But you do not stop
for your child at school. You telephone your husband
from the house. He stammers yes,
he'll stop for the boy.

Ten minutes pass. You notice that the sun across the street
is about to fall backwards off a neighbor's roof.
You think of the yard work to do, and the small splinter
which just yesterday you dug from your palm with a needle.

But the reddish spot does not keep you
from taking out the rake again, fitting your breath
to the rhythm of your arms, your thighs. With every tug
on the handle you feel a little more sure.

This is how I would like to leave you: thinking
that when your husband comes you will hug him,
you will clamp your son to you, but will not cry.
At this time of the year, even the trees have lumps

high in their limbs—the brown nests, abandoned circles.
"Yes. I am no different," you say through clenched teeth.
Across the street a neighbor starts waving,
thinking you are calling to him.

Wing Span

The thin skin I hoist against this weather,
the vulture presence of my collapsible umbrella,
sulks in the corner of the room. The drips

from its beak and black slickened feathers
remind me that I too am a victim
of what falls from the sky. Standing on one leg

my umbrella preens itself through the night.
As I lift up its weight next morning, the folds
have already rubbed themselves pure. Trembling

it flies from the perch on my arm, falcon ready
to smite all beasts of land and air
to avenge the blindness it has suffered

before I tug away its hood.

Two Poems

Blue lawn chair, blue flower,
the splash of the wading pool

through the sliding screen door, maybe

on Venus, a life for me. Somewhere,
in small returnable bottles,

in the small blue fingers of capillaries,

there is a life for me, blue
as a blue bicycle—and you, standing there

laugh at the poem I am scribbling

on the rough grain of this table, the splintered
valleys of the blue planet we inhabit. No,

not blue, unless seen so far away in space

that it no longer matters.
But it does matter. No need for apologies, no need

for us to disagree with the tug of gravity—and

if we decide to levitate, what will we become,
some poor priest

who can't love the rivers

in his local parish, who hears confession through
the hard grate of his career?

Now or Never

Yellow bananas, yellow bowl, the faint
blue moon of desire. All that I understand

I understand now. The refrigerator magnet
clutching our most important words.

The horizon bending like the sharp corners of the sink.
In the back yard the mud

is singing flat.

Nota Bene

Yes, there is the street outside, the white street
reddening, the whip of lights as an ambulance

heads down Beall Avenue, blows its horn and clears the intersection.
Yes, there is snow, and

it keeps on falling, piling up
the dirty slush of numbers. Death

and its rumored versions. But from here
it just looks calm, a benediction

to a very hard year—so bad
my wife won't be coming home. So I sit here, reading,

the final words of my students, the Christmas tree lights
giving off discreet signals. The angel on the tree

spreading out her wings,
poised to swaddle or to flog.

Beside the Road

The man gets down from his tractor
because he has seen his wife
step out on the edge of the soft ploughed field.
There is no need to know

why she needs him. He walks towards her,
with each step they sink ankle-deep
in the upturned earth, then rise again
as if walking towards each other naked

on the mattress of their bed.
Soon, they will be close enough to talk, not talk.
Maybe their hands will clasp. I don't know,
I'll be too far away to see them. All this

has happened out my window. I turn
to describe it to my wife, but there is too much
ground between us already, too much contradiction
for the story I would like to tell.

III. I Hold My Family

I Hold My Family

The terrified birds
forsook their roof-top nests in helplessness,
but you were still more helpless than the birds,
for you had no wings
and knew not where to fly.
—Jaroslav Seifert

The Gutenberg Bible, ca. 1454, first book printed from
movable type, is available for use by the public, but must be
given to the patron only under the close supervision of a
full-time staff member who will be responsible for opening
the book, turning the pages, and any other physical manipu-
lation of the volume.
—Lilly Library Reading Room Manual,
Indiana University

I: *The Reading Room*
   High ceilings, worn carpet the color
of my blue dishwash soap, the color
      of the veins on my legs.
         & there must be real butternut
      in that panelling,
   the pale color of the doors of our old house.

   I might be at home here too,
but the books in the room all point out
   from the wall at me, their colored spines
         shrill to my eyes,
      asking why I am here. Everything

wants to keep me from my Gutenberg,
      its black martyred skin,
   "first book ever printed,"
said the newspaper, & so I came in,
      feeling gawky, wondering if I dressed right

to read the Bible that was given
straight from the hand of God,
his voice pouring uncontrollable
into my ear.

But this young male librarian will not leave me
alone with my message. He stays here,
fussing with his hands, with this card
he makes me fill out. He should be

awed & blinded, made to go away
by the red & green paintings
on each page, the big colored letters
which will tell my history to me, the big
red & green colors, mixed in the juices
of man & woman,
Phil & me.

This young man calls it *rubrication.*
Strange sound which slips on my tongue.
Every letter in this book is a curling figure
whispering to me like a fire. Even the black

book's black cover talks as I caress it.
I have that gift from God. But the librarian
won't let me hold the book by myself. I plead with him:
"Don't you see each of the nails,
driven down through the leather, tells a story
of what Phil did to me. Here is my son & his birth
& here is my mother laid. Here is what daddy said
but I didn't listen & here
is my skin stretched in Phil's arms till it hardened
with age & began to hurt." Still the young man

won't let me touch it. He turns
the pages too quickly, won't let me watch
the slow pain of my life go by.
I should tell him more plainly
why this book means so much to me.

"See, here is the P— here
    is the huge O decorated
in a tiny silk webbing. So much care.
My hand could work one like that, the lattice
    of pale red & blue lines in the O.
These must never be broken, for they are the egg,
    the ovum. . .

        The B. There it is! B is for that bastard.
    The son of a bitch did it to me. Bitch-bastard.
        Do you understand? Phil is on this page.
    Bitch-bastard—" The young male librarian

        says I cannot curse in here. But he
    calms down & turns the page, asking
me continually when I will be finished.
        How can I tell? Everything goes
    so awkwardly with his arm barring
        the book so I cannot feel it,
    its black, knowing skin.

        But I can see each page— turn, turn.
The P, the O. "P is for Phil, the initial
    who fills me, the egg, the O. A is for Anna,
        my middle name. T is for Tom, our only boy."
        The book shows us as God wanted
        & I forget I'm talking out loud
        & again the librarian tells me
not to moan so loud in here.

II: *The Pigeons*

    & all at once they take
        my book away from me.
I have walked here dreading each step
    on the wet sidewalks
        the mud under my feet
            squishing

like my diaphragm
when I filled it with foam
& folded it like a slippery half-moon
& slid it into me
& then Phil didn't come home.

& today the pigeons underneath the awnings
watched me & the rain as it fell
& they raised up in the air & banked
& settled by my feet.

They cautioned: "Don't go! Phil
has stopped by already
and warned them you are coming."

But I had to come—
despite their percolating voices
busy with mourning
their continual fluster
at the helplessness of flight
when they have to watch their nests

scraped out from under the eaves.
They hear each clump of straw
scattered on the pavement—
& the slow oozing from their broken eggs,
the giving way of shells
& rupture of the yellow membrane within.

& each day I tell them I want
to hear— as they hear—
ever since they appeared unto me
in the cold shiny pages of the National Geographic
at the clinic
as I sat chipping at the paint on my nails
& the bits collected
in the middle of the book
spread open on my lap. As I turned

each page inside the yolk-colored covers
    I felt how slick & clean
was the surface
    slick & clean
      as the tools
the doctors used
when they took away my womb.

    & I want to hear as they heard—

Floating high above the hills
    near our old home in Solsberry
they heard the low-frequency moan
    from the Gulf of Mexico,
    the wave crawling up on shore
on Galveston Beach where we had our honeymoon.

    & at the same time
they stored in their heads the echo
    of the surf off Hatteras
where Tom would be stationed
    & at the same time they heard
the steady fall of snow on the Rockies
where Phil promised we would go.

& all along Phil complained
    there were too many pigeons.
As they flew off the barn
    he shot them

    & his blue-tick bird dog Hank
buried his head deep in their feathers
    fetched them back to the porch
opened the wet rubber edges of his mouth
    & dropped them near my feet.

    & now this male librarian also
wants to cut away part of my life.

"A quarter to five," he warns. I wince
as he slides the book off the table
& into his other arm. "Please be careful,"
I say. "Do you know how to carry it?"

He looks at me & the clock
& intones like a preacher
"We must take the Gutenberg to the vault now,"
& he points me to the door.
He wants to shoo me out.
The padded door unlocks with a click
I feel between my legs.

III: *I Hold My Family*

Soon the surf on the Pacific
will hatch in my ears
break beneath my body
as I hear across two thousand miles
my Phil check the nests of Portland Oregon
& mingling with his whispers
the lapping of baywater
on the pilings of the wharves, the soft
spongy noise of the bedsprings
as when he bird-dogged Bev Frawley
at her pre-fab in Elletsville
& bought whiskey & beer
to last them both the night
& used up our life savings
a little bit each time.

& now there's nothing for me to do
but to go home— listen
for the thrash of waves
foaming over on top of themselves
before they even start to travel
in from the open sea.

If I could have held
a little while longer
that black bible skin to my skin
I could have listened
& heard more than what can be summed by words.

I could hear Phil as he snores by a woman.
I could hear Tommy turning over
in a room full of sleeping Marines.
I thrash in my blankets, over
& over upon myself. But I
must do the listening for them all.
I hold my family,

so how can I sleep?
I feel the bed beneath me shake,
the electricity from my heart
running to the floor. No use
to hold my thighs, my hips & arms rigid,
it would only make the room rock
more swiftly, make it harder
to bear when my nightmare comes—
when even the pigeons are not my friends.

& I see the work that Phil
did to the Gutenberg,
how he smeared on fake shapes
to lead me astray,
tainting with his own juice
the holy whiteness of the leaves.

—how he reached the doctor's
before I did, planted the National Geographic
in the middle of the rack. Maybe the pigeons
have always loved him more.

But I feel no blame
no reproach for them as I hear

their nervous flutter & soft chilly cry
from their narrow stone shelves
above the library door
as they watch him enter
beneath their plump, aching legs. In that library
there is every issue of every magazine
until back before the war
& he has come to browse through their secrets
like he thumbed through mine.

& they know he's inside, laughing
& his laugh
breaks against their heads.
The parts of the nests inside them
wash away with every brush of his voice
across their smooth stretches
of feather & tensed-up skin. Their cherry
red claws still aching for his back
they flop at the glass again & again.
To reach him, they would
fly through walls a foot thick
if only through walls
he would softly call their names.

IV. Our Own Fragile Paths

To A Woman Mauled in Yellowstone

She did everything wrong. She was alone:
slept in the clothes she cooked in, entered
the back country while menstruating. For miles
a bear can smell human sexual activity,
says the brochure, and we must be careful
to lock all the food in the trunk. In seconds
they can tear open an ice chest.

When walking bear territory, make noise,
tie pans and spoons to your waist
and sing as you go. Let them know you are here.
Keep up wind. Let them smell you, decide
if they want to make the encounter. After all
it is their land, and if they single you out
you have already made your mistake.

Climb a tree or play dead. If you run
it will only excite them. It is always
the victim's fault. We bang her name
to make a loud noise between us
until, safe in the car,
we can say there is no harm
to feed these big lugs sweets
or call them Yogi, that perverted
childhood beast with vest, necktie and hat,
but no pants.

Cleaning Out the Nest

—itself without eyes, but containing young with eyes
well-developed.
    —caption under a photograph of a dissected
Cuban Blind Fish (*Lucifuga*), prepared by C. H.
Eigenmann, Indiana University, ca. 1904.

Lapped on top of each
other's backs, the babies
in the Cuban Blind Fish's
split-open belly
all have eyes. Their bodies touch
like hands offered in prayer
from all sides of a table.
a white table, well lit.

As we pull each one out,
sorting through the tangle
inside the pouch where a mother's
cramped up creating takes place,
a slippery explosion,
the bloating and puncturing
of sacs in cavities,

the graphic cant of church billboards
remains in the back of the mind, the myth
against opening doors in the body,
the horror of salt serum and plastic bag.
But here in Biology 101, the smell
on our fingers revolts us the most,
the gag of formaldehyde clings
to our memory
long after our study jars are pitched.

Holding nothing sacred, living forms
do dirty work to survive.
Even the womb tampers with its young,

absorbing back into itself the eyes
which had already sprouted, closing up
the prayer of flesh for light. "All
is palimpsest—" the buildup of chalk
from the last class to use the blackboard
wiped over and over with a dirty rag.

Still lingering on our tongues, the taste
from the walls of our mothers, the variations
of fire, earth,
water and air. Into new terrain
we stick out feelers, the annex needed
for experiments, the next hybrids of temptation
we keep pulling from the vine. We cry
more light so our children
can at least glimpse
the same animals we faced
spread before us on the table
like an open page.

Bottom Fish

Problems confront the deep sea fishes.
In their vertical commute
they withstand great swings of pressure.
Since in the cold and dark there is little use
in swimming, best off are those with bone and muscle
poorly developed. Only a few ever touch bottom.

Those who live to tell the tale
to the world on top explode— their guts
forced out of their mouths by the ruptured
fundamental peace of their bladders.
Something like this happens when a father
takes a gun down the darkened hall
to his son's room, his daughter's, and so on,
to save them from the depths in which he struggles.
Then he leaves a note
as if reading the contents of his stomach
were not enough.

Sex, of course, is difficult anywhere on earth.
But below the first six hundred meters
the chances of meeting flesh are slender,
no matter what your intentions. Thus, various
specializations have evolved, including
the body organs responsible for light,
patterns stippled along the sides and belly
like a neon advertisement. Each species
has its own marquee. With so few mates available,
it would be a shame to approach
from the wrong end, or too quickly.

                              Now for my story.
Two fish are swimming towards each other
in the abysmal plains not far
from the beaches for which Florida is famous.

One dangles a luminous, fleshy bulb from the tip
of its transparent fin, on the make for easy prey.
The other, the frugal burgher viperfish,
knows that no food, even bigger than he,
can be wasted. Fangs thin as the ribs
of some minnows, he latches on to the pulsing bud
and dislocates his jaw, waiting for the proposal
to be accepted, for the dark festivities to begin.

Hunters Are Magnificent Animals

Blowing clumps of deer
onto nearby tree bark
hunters are magnificent animals.
We find them a challenge. After all,
they are more than just dumb beasts.
One can run without his heart for minutes.
Shoot one in the stomach
and he will last for days.

Folks say they've tracked back
to the bottomland in numbers
rutting it up with their pickups all spring.
If you hide well enough
you can spot them
bend down to inspect a kill.
Now, while they take it easy,
bag them
as you watch their red vests swell.

Or surprise one in the headlights
and have a gun in the back.
No one will ever know
how you snagged this beauty for your wall.
A pot belly does not make
for good eating. True.
But his dumb loving eyes
stare a blessing for your home.
Your children call him "uncle."
They wipe the dust from off his ears.

Aunt Linda Speaks

Each summer we come to Kentucky Lake and finally
we buy a pontoon house boat, show my cat Snow White

what can be seen in the water. Her claws dig in
to my arms,

leave feverish scratches,
and I put her down quick.

Yes, my fur can get raised too, raised up high, hackled.
My name is Aunt Linda and my nephew

is the one who wrote what you and I
are reading. Look how easy it is for him

to remember the sharp squeak of styrofoam on the 1960
Nixon for President hat he carried. Five years old, he

was helping me move back home from my two-room apartment
in the Goosenibble section of Olney, Illinois,

an apartment I still dream about and the apartment
still dreams about me,

my fingers digging at the mattress, while
my twins Tommy and Tonya were created, and now

this nephew writes a poem
as if sense will be made

as if never asking his mother to this day
who the father was

or even asking me
was better than my having to stare

floating out here
in the middle of Kentucky Lake

where others can see
what I'm reading.

Gleaning the Field (1973)

The cold sun melts
into the horizon, nudging
the trees. I struggle
along the cornrow. My foot
crushes holes in the glaze,
the ice over toppled stalks.
Early December, the field
under water the entire fall,
our John Deere unable
to muck its way through,
we are here to glean
the corn before it rots.

Last night Dave and I drove
to the Airport Inn near Vincennes,
came back by the Wabash bottoms,
froze two deer in our headlights
when we turned into a field.
As they loped off we started
on the remains of the six-pack
leaning our elbows on the roof of the car.

I've been out here eight hours.
At last my dad's back gives out
and we quit. Up on the wagon,
I hoist my aching weight, lift
the entire day, every basket
I have had to empty, the rasp
on my palms of each kernel
that has worked its way through my gloves.
Any moment now, and my hangover
will evaporate. Each cob will yield
a chunk of gold, each bushel
an amber pitcher. These hours
will have gone down like water.

Bad Roads

Her knees made her feel like
she walked on stilts. She
left a few coins on the table by her cup.

She fumbled in her purse to find her keys.
The wheel didn't seem
to be attached to her hands. Her front end

slid toward the centerline. She eased herself
to a stop, checked the mailbox, felt
pain snake the length of her arm. Next day

she called in sick. It was too far
on roads like these. She cooked
more food than she could eat.

The Cost of the Image

The C plus
I received for painting

stars in a snowy sky. My third grade teacher
stringing fence

between me and the impossible.
Or my mother, when she asserted

wolves roam the tender
extended haunch of Illinois

while I sneered they were only coyote,
flunking the woman that gave me birth.

Or you, brushing
the edge of this poem, picking up the splinter

of metaphor. Your lips
mercurochrome red, mouthing the wound of speech.

All the Philosophies in the World

When does haze become fog, when
does tree beget forest? I look out

at the Vermilion River,
the slow bend of its arm

like an old lady trailing her hand, yes,
slowly,

through the dust beside her bed
on a night too hot to sleep. Think

of the deer in her closet. It's a dream,
really, and she rises up, not quite able

to tear
herself from the humid

web we all

lie down to
not quite

sure if the deer
are tangled in her clothes, if the

phone is ringing. If it might
be me, her son.

Did You Know

A snake is warmer than you think?
If you take his temperature
you will find him
a very dry eighty eight degrees.

Even a snail
is seventy six degrees and an oyster
eighty two.

The snake by now is wiser
is underneath a log
his tongue erasing at the edge
of his shadow, waiting,

and will not come out. This snake.
No matter how long
you keep from breathing.
No matter how long you remain.

But you realize he is too close to the house.
If you walk away he will follow.
You're sure his skin has grown colder,
is slimy, and your gaze
is all that keeps him from sliding up your leg.

You freeze
but already you start thinking back. Did you
take that snake's temperature or not?
Was it a dream,

what are you flushing out and why?
Who brought up snakes
and where is the hoe?

                              (after W. C. W.)

The Rainbow Sheep

this boy has slept between us till he's almost
in first grade the charley-horse kid his grandpa
calls him I tell you it ain't funny the boy
comes in whining with the leg ache can we smear
some smelly linament on him soon he wants
to tuck his leg in under yours we can't move
for fear we'd crush his bones I say he's prying
apart what we've slapped together for a home

there is no animal in the world like that

Sunday mornings he pads in his animal
coloring book open to the snakes he's done
in all thirty-two crayolas he'd be dumb
enough to paint a snake he saw in the yard
I took away the book horses with blue tails
and green haunches red udders on the milk cows
a purple-yellow zebra dog he never
uses brown like he's been told to do for fur

there is no animal in the world like that

I'm at work he noses around in my shed
and takes things from where I put them I have no
good tools left I have to wait for you to put
him to bed so I can go and set things straight
I always hate to see the moon when it's full
too much light I see furrows in its face it's
too much like the boy's face the time he followed
me out with a toy flashlight and I hit him

Virginia Woolf's Half-Sister, Laura

Another Sunday, I am left at home, the fires
in the parlor snuffed out. I speak
when everyone is gone. Fondling
the toys in the nursery, I touch
each gift they first gave to her: the gallant
rocking horse, or the badly-stuffed clown
shoved in my lap my twenty-first birthday.
Yes, I know what gifted means: Virginia's words
strewn like powder throughout the rooms. Once
she found me while I sat on the floor and rocked
my own body as if it were a doll. Her voice,
each syllable, tangled in the roots of my hair.
She said *you are a tree, leafed for summer,*
deaf to all the world but the rain.

Etude in Black and White

Bare shoulders, buttocks, the moon,
coils of fog draped around the high hills,
the rise and fall of ground, a twisting path
slowly climbed, the vines cleared with a tug.

I see you, don't see you. I climb,
don't climb. I think of your wrists, your ankles,
the harshness of bark and the sticky white lines
where the ants always crawl.

We breathe each other's air. The trees breathe,
the birds relieved I have not come for them, breathe.
Already the moon goes hollow, dark. The fog
climbs high above it through the trees. Shoulders,

buttocks disappear. The fish at your feet
disappear, diving from the surface of the pond.
The last thing you see: their lips pouting; open and close,
open and close; the outgoing rings; a flicker of skin.

In This World, Light . . .

Imagine you are the blindfish, the cave-
excursion boat drawing near, the glow
from the lantern like a sudden bump
against your white lips. You tremble

during each of these sudden visitations,
the thrust and suction of the oars
on the water—a surface as delicate
as your own transparent skin. The boat

passes over; you feel the raw wash
of waves on the blood in your gills.
Imagine these gills as your tingling fingers
groping the depths of a darkened room.

The Tree That Remains

I
Tilting out over water,
a tree cannot control its footing,
and belly flops into the by-wash, but
too heavy to float, it collapses
down toward the deep middle,
and comes to rest
on the bottom
by the weight of earth
clinging to its root tangle.

The ball of dirt and wood
is firmly stuck to the mud bed,
and for months, the trunk
and all its limp, shaggy limbs
nod slowly in the current,
murmuring, as the river
calmly strips off the leaves,
and chews them, softens in its wet mouth
the smaller branches until
they are black and spongy,
with strips of bark barely hanging,
the decaying feathers of future silt.

II
But, years later,
as you navigate the river,
look out for the tree that remains,
a dark jagged skeleton
whose prongs point upward,
the wood swollen and hard.

The more powerful the engine,
the deeper the gash in the hull.
In this world, wood takes vengeance
on wood. Imagine as you glide
painstakingly over this region,
on the lookout
for the swirls over snags,

imagine your own arms
held outward
in constant, gracious blessing
for the bending of the river,
which destroys you,
eats away the bank,
and then whittles you down
to your hardest elements.
Imagine now your own hands,

inches from the surface,
over which living things still pass.
Can you restrain them? There is a time
for sadness, yes, but also a tightening
which comes to the skin, the preparation
for the making of new destruction.

Go slowly over these waters
so that you might look down
and see your own dark face
staring up. If you are careful,
it will not keep you
when you are ready to leave.
Remember you have the gift
of floating. Remember you have friends
on the banks.

Wreath

The wreath went one step further than the hair-ring,
woven from the locks of a young lady and usually given to
her fiance.

        —Victorians by Artifact

Gaudy in a way. In a way somber. A tale of death
to sit through on a visit. This is the attraction of swarm,
the ritual of scissors and a mother peering at our scalp.
Over a tub screened from view by the barn, young girls
weeded out the locks busy fingers wove on sticky nights
steeped in the smell of kerosene. Time twining with motion,
too much faith in their hands, they stretched short lives
into families, into blossoms intimate and tangling.
At the center, child hair twisted into the bunched sex
of stamen and pistil, the sleeping with a brother
before the first guilty knowledge of the body.
In the outer calyx, tight curlicues of adult tension,
the pushing back against his thrust in bed, over supper,
over the failings of a child.

                              Would they have slackened—
Penelopes who spent their lives to wind and unwind
each other's hair—if they knew it was I who would take them
away from this house emptied of bedsteads, the black piano
and etched porcelain cups, anything of use to the modern
daughter's home? Only the mud-daubers remained
to share in the coming of the bulldozer
to my grandmother's house; and I, a strange savior,

have no better tradition, no other Old World.
Both family and foreign, each strand an icon in progress,
bound covenant, frayed diaspora. And I can never
look at it a second time, without seeing
a completely different woman, a different death,
a different lover, there, unravelling,

undressing before me, stiff in the moonlight,
unravelling in a call of distress that I
might never understand her quick, her center,
her girl-pulp hardening to ancestor,
her frazzle that comes from being woven too tight.

Once Again

Stretching my body against the back of your body,
the small salty rivers popping up between us
as we immerse in the brackishness of the first summer night
we have spent together in so long,
                              the first few tugs
of a freight train's moaning whistle
travel the slow seven miles from town
like a son drunk and unsure
of his hands on the wheel, of his feet on gravel,
pulling two or three times on our screen door
before it opens.

81

Goodbye to the Poetry of James Wright Elegies

Having harnessed the horse of brief words
and the smooth-running engine
of the Ohio River,

Having come to His unadorned plot—
a hometown of fast food, bank branches,
the chain link fence of a closed factory—

We stand here, below freezing,
to drink and piss by the Great Poet's Grave,
to watch our own rivers start their fragile paths.

From a Shipyard in a Bottle

A bird can break his beak doing this kind of work.
—Gdańsk, author unknown

piece by piece
a crane was assembled
flapping above a dock
squeaking from lack of grease
lack of feathers and fertilized eggs
picking up other hard pieces
building a nest of ships

but who put it in this bottle

it took the patient hands of a general
their armored fingertips
maneuvering for the buttons of the enemy
it took the practiced hands of a banker
which know the weight of brick and meat
which know how to sweep a landscape off the table
and leave buildings and goblets in place

you can imagine

looking out from any kind of bottle
the distortion
the thought that we're a message to the world

well here's the crumpled paper

this is a bottle
whose neck gets narrower
outward our claws keep stretching
made of steel
though we can't break through
they tell us *build*
build ships

ships sailing outside
the jagged edges of our necks

In Which I Share a Gull's Knowledge of Rivers

Across the river, boat docks, white boats and sand,
the reflecting chalk sides of high-rises,
further north, the fish underbelly of the bridge,
and all this glaring light
on the one gull floating downriver.

The bird is oblivious. Asleep,
a white Cleopatra on the Vistula,
it lounges, head barely erect, until nearing
the concrete pylons of Lazienkowski Bridge,
it slowly, lazily
flaps its white scarves,
lifting its pampered body
for the short flight back upstream.

I am too far away to hear the splash,
but I see the bird tuck in its wings,
relax on the blue barge of summer.
All of this work to stay in one place.

(*Warsaw, June 1983*)